THE GIFT OF WISDOM

(encouragement for the soul)

BY: DONNA SIMS
INNER BEAUTY MINISTRIES

The Gift of Wisdom

Copyright © 2024 by Donna Sims

All rights reserved. Neither this book, nor any parts within it may be sold or reproduced in any form or by any electronic or mechanical means, including information storage and retrieval systems, without permission in writing from the author. The only exception is by a reviewer, who may quote short excerpts in a review.

Library of Congress Control Number: 978166294776

ISBN (paperback): 9781662947766
eISBN: 9781662947773

Table of Contents

Introduction	6
Getting over Hurt	8
Attitude of Gratitude	10
The Truth about Fear	12
Listen to Your Intuition	15
Control Issues	17
Believe in Miracles	19
It Takes Discipline	21
Embrace Change	23
Be Mindful of Your Thoughts	25
Be True to Yourself	27
Decision Making	29
Dark Energies	31
Spending Time Alone	33
Divine Intervention	35
Soul Family vs. Blood Family	37
Honest Communication	39
Set Clear Boundaries	41
Examine Yourself	43
Hurt People, Hurt People	45

Breaking Generational Curses	47
Seed Time and Harvest	49
There is More than Enough	51
A Guilty Conscience	53
Don't Be Greedy	55
Feelings of Jealousy	57
Taking Accountability	59
Enabling Is Not Helping	61
Surrender	63
Ask for Help	65
Self-Sabotage	67
Making Assumptions	69
People Pleasing	71
Ego	73
Trusting Others	75
Dealing with Temptation	77
Compassion for Others	79
Illusions	81
Follow the Path Given to You	83
Dealing with Difficult People	85
Be Intentional	87
Conclusion	90

Introduction

Hello, my name is Donna Sims, and I am the founder of Inner Beauty Ministries. I am an intuitive empath, which simply means I am sensitive to other people's energetic field. I am strongly led by my intuition to understand a situation. As a certified energy healer, I primarily help people identify mental blockages that affect their spiritual growth and provide knowledge and tools on how to remove those blockages. My mission is to provide healing for a happier, healthier, and more peaceful life.

I believe that we are all connected and the people that you meet in this lifetime are not by chance. Everyone who reads this book is meant to find it. This tells me that there will be something for you or someone that you are connected to in this book. The information is strictly my opinion and based on several factors including my relationship with God, my friendships, my familial and romantic relationships, my clients, and my spiritual teachings.

As I reflect on my life, I am grateful for every obstacle that I have faced. The key to rising above the obstacles in this life is to see things from a higher perspective. Your vision must be greater than what you have experienced and can physically see. Your happiness truly does come from within.

The book is written from the perspective of identifying and overcoming everyday issues that have the potential to hinder your spiritual growth. Each chapter offers a short summary and only covers one aspect of the subject. There is definitely more discussion to be had. Not everything in life is black and white. There is a lot of grey area, and each circumstance varies, so please consider that when applying the principles within this book. While I have included bible references, I don't consider this a Christian book because no matter your religion or background, you will be able to relate to the content. Keep in mind that we will not see change in our lives unless we make a conscious decision to change it.

THANK YOU FOR
SUPPORTING MY BOOK.
For additional questions or concerns,
please email me at
innerbeautyminllc@gmail.com
or visit my website at
www.innerbeautyshines.com.

Getting Over Hurt

At some point in life, you will deal with someone who has hurt you. This hurt includes someone lying to you, saying hurtful words, or betraying your trust. It's unfortunate and doesn't feel good. Try not to internalize the pain to the point that you feel victimized. Someone's subpar actions are more about their issues than they are about yours. It is your responsibility to pull yourself up and get out of that negative energy because it can lead to resentfulness, depression, overthinking, anger, and even stagnation in your life. You are here to grow and prosper in this life. The goal is to not let someone else's actions affect who you are or how you show up in the world. Yes, it will take some time to process your feelings and that is perfectly okay, but please be mindful that feelings of being hurt can take a negative turn if you linger on the pain.

Tips:

1. Tell the person who hurt you how you feel about what happened, especially if the relationship with this person is one that you value. Speak your truth with kindness. Try to focus on your feelings and not what they did.
2. Have faith and believe that this will pass. You will move past this.
3. Forgive them. Forgiving someone is not for the other person; it is for you. It is for you because you are taking responsibility for your own happiness and emotional state of being. When you forgive those who have wronged you, good things will happen for you. Remember God sees all things.
4. Stop reliving the hurt. This means to stop continually talking about what they did. When you talk about it over and over, it's hard to move on from the emotional pain. Instead, find positive activities to do instead.
5. Do not retaliate. By retaliating, you give power to those who have hurt you.

Scripture references:

Ephesians 6:16, Mark 11:25, Matthew 5:43-45

Attitude of Gratitude

It is extremely important to have a good attitude even in times of adversity. Trying times are temporary, not permanent. In times of despair, always look beyond where you are because "this too shall pass." Smiling, being friendly, and speaking positively are all ways to show gratitude. We all long to believe in something greater than ourselves, so keep the faith and believe that things will get better. Studies show that when we stay positive, we attract more positive things into our lives. Gratitude is the key to manifesting happiness, abundance, and prosperity.

Tips:

1. Choose gratitude. Every day thank God, the Creator, for choosing you to be here in existence.
2. Journal. Write down the things that you are grateful for and focus on those things.
3. Stay positive. You may not be where you want to be, but you are alive, and with every new day comes a new opportunity.

Scripture references:

Jeremiah 29:11, Romans 8:28, Philippians 4:4-7

THE TRUTH ABOUT FEAR

The definition of fear is an unpleasant emotion caused by the *belief* that someone or something is dangerous, likely to cause pain, or a threat. Most of us have fears because of a traumatic event that we have endured in our past or because a future situation looks unfamiliar to us. Some examples are being afraid to fall in love again because your last relationship ended in heartbreak, attending college at an older age, or making a career change because you don't know what to expect. Either way, your fears are rooted in something that is not in your current reality.

The truth is that you don't know how things will turn out, so it is imperative to stay faithful. Also, being fearful leads to overthinking and sometimes we can talk ourselves out of the very thing that we truly desire. Know that you will have to take a risk and make some sacrifices to elevate to new levels.

This can be scary, but the reward will be worth it. There is a famous quote that says, "You must do things you have never done in order to get things you have never had." I am here to encourage you to believe in a power greater than your eyes can see.

Tips:

1. Control your thinking. Whenever you find yourself thinking negatively or thinking the worst of a situation, immediately turn that thought around into a positive one.
2. Have faith. With discipline and determination, along with your faith, you will succeed. With faith, all things are possible.
3. Stay present. Yesterday is gone, and tomorrow is not here. By staying in the present moment, you can see what is needed today to reach your goals.
4. Stay positive. Positiveness is directly related to your faith. What you want, wants you.
5. Determine whether something is an actual threat or a perceived threat. Your fears can distort your perception of reality.

Disclaimer: All things must be put into perspective, of course, because some things are dangerous for us and do cause harm and pain. Please seek professional help if that is the case.

Scripture references:

Deuteronomy 31:6, Philippians 4:6-7, Psalm 23:4

LISTEN TO YOUR INTUITION

The beautiful thing about being spiritual is that God has equipped you with intuition. Have you ever been in a situation where something felt "off," or maybe in a situation where something felt "right?" That feeling is your intuition. It is an inner knowing—one that cannot be explained but can always be trusted. If an anticipated offer is presented to you that appears promising, but for some reason, you can't escape the feeling that you should reject the offer, that is your intuition. Your intuition guides you and will repeatedly send you confirmation about a person or situation. It is God's sacred gift to you, rooted in love. It is important to have quiet time, pay attention, and listen to that small still voice.

Tips:

1. Trust your gut feeling.
2. Your intentions and thoughts are two different things. Your thoughts are from your mind, but your intuition is from your spirit. The goal is to calm the mind and trust your spirit.
3. Do not argue with anyone about or try to convince them of what your intuition has shown you.

Scripture references:

Romans 8:14, Proverbs 2:6, John 16:13

Control Issues

One way to know if you have control issues is to pay attention to the relationship you have with yourself and others. Do you insist on having things your way instead of giving others the freedom to be themselves? Control prevents growth, and growth is necessary for personal development. Controlling behavior stems from a sense of powerlessness, fear, and insecurities that make you feel vulnerable. This vulnerability creates the need to control situations to feel safe. Control causes resistance, and resistance is the quickest way to hinder manifestation. When faced with people or situations that are not on the same page as you, take a step back and let whatever happens happen. When you disconnect from the outcome of a situation, you open yourself up to receiving more than you could have imagined.

Tips:

1. Take advantage of opportunities for advancement, even if it reminds you of a previous failed attempt.
2. Make choices out of love by being understanding.
3. Be authentic in how you express yourself and more of the same will come to you.
4. Give someone the freedom to choose rather than make the choice for them.

Scripture references:

2 Timothy 1:7, Romans 16:17-18, Hebrews 11:1

Believe in Miracles

Your divine existence is not by accident. You are here for a reason and purpose, so embrace this life and give the world the best of you. Trust that our Creator is omnipotent, omnipresent, and omniscient. Not only the creation of human beings but the millions of species of plants and animals in our world speak to the presence of miracles. There are many things that you will not be able to comprehend with your finite mind such as unexplained healings or deaths, premonitions, psychic powers, and synchronicities. Therefore, don't find it strange when things that you hope and wish for do not happen as there is a time and place for everything. Remember, there is a higher power at play.

Tips:

1. Have faith and believe in what seems impossible.
2. Think big because we serve a big God.
3. Continue moving forward with your dreams even when setbacks occur.

Scripture references:

Jeremiah 32:27, Job 5:8-9, Ephesians 3:20

It Takes Discipline

Whether it's that dream job you want that you never applied for, that relationship you want that you haven't invested in, that business you want that you haven't started, or even reinventing yourself, it all takes discipline. Acknowledging the desires of your heart is the first step. Second, you must make a conscious decision to move towards that aspiration. As stated in another chapter, you were chosen and created with characteristics especially for you. Trust your intuition but know that if you don't explore your talents, then you will only have the idea of your dreams. Procrastination will come in the form of excuses with the most common one being, "It's not the right time." The truth is that it will never be the right time; just do it. You must be dedicated and work hard to make your dreams a reality.

Tips:

1. Conduct research on the very thing that you desire. Being knowledgeable will boost your confidence.
2. Don't make excuses as to why you can't or haven't done it. We all make time for the things we truly want to do.
3. Watch out for opposing forces—negative thoughts and negative people. Cast down negative thoughts. Some people will not want to see you succeed; surround yourself with positive people for encouragement.
4. Plan and dedicate time, even a small amount of time daily, to achieving your goal.

Scripture references:

Hebrews 12:11, 2 Timothy 1:7, Proverbs 15:32

Embrace Change

Change is inevitable and with change comes growth. You will encounter different people and situations on your life's journey. A person's rate of change depends on many factors, including their friends and family, environment, and way of thinking. It's important to keep an open mind and a positive perspective regarding the challenges of life. Everything that happens is ultimately for your good, even if you can't see it in your current situation. The key is to stay focused on the things that you want, not the things that you don't want. During times of transformation, uncertainties will arise, but you must push through to reach the other side. You will make it. If you were to think back over the past ten years, most of you have gone through some life-changing events, including marriages, divorces, breakups, new jobs, or financial challenges.

New decisions must be made, and maybe in the past, you could relate to a situation or circumstance that now makes you feel out of place. Unfortunately, as we evolve, we have no choice but to leave certain people, places, or things behind because it does not align with who we are anymore. This time is no different. It's all a part of the process. Trust the process.

Tips:

1. Periodically, sit down and take inventory of your life; identify and take steps to separate yourself from things that no longer serve you.
2. Give yourself grace during this time of transition. It will feel uncomfortable. It's called "growing pains" for a reason.
3. Trust in your ability to decide what's best for you.
4. Move toward that which speaks to your soul.

Scripture references:

1 Corinthians 13:11, Deuteronomy 31:6, Romans 12:2

Be Mindful of Your Thoughts

If you have endured a situation that has negatively affected your thinking, it is imperative to heal from that situation, or you will subconsciously create a negative footprint in your mind. It will not only affect you but those that are connected to you as well. For instance, you can think that a helpful person is too good to be true simply because you are accustomed to dealing with people who take advantage of you. Furthermore, you can cause others to be suspicious of that person; all for no good reason. It is easy for your thoughts to run away with you. Pessimism invites anxiety, stress, and a lack of trust. The ability to see a situation in a positive light is reflective of your faith; therefore, believe that everything happens for a reason. People with a more optimistic outlook are more likely to take advantage of opportunities with the belief that the change will result in a favorable outcome.

The interpretation of your circumstances is a matter of perspective.

Tips:

1. Whenever a negative thought comes into your mind, immediately cast it down and replace it with a positive thought.
2. Don't advise others based on your own negative thinking.
3. Try to find the good in every situation.
4. Surround yourself with positive people.

Scripture references:

Philippians 4:8, Proverbs 4:23-24, Romans 8:28

BE TRUE TO YOURSELF

Do you find yourself hiding who you really are out of fear of being hurt, taken advantage of, or others' opinions of you? If so, then you are not living your truth. It is important to take time to get to know yourself and what truly makes you happy. Following your happiness and expressing yourself increases your self-esteem. For instance, if you are surrounded by people who exhibit harmful lifestyle choices, such as excessive drinking, promiscuity, or overall complacency, that do not align with the life you want, you will need to create boundaries and only participate in the activities that make you feel comfortable. A strong sense of self may sometimes intimidate others, and that is okay. On the other hand, by not operating according to your truth, you only disappoint yourself. Authentically showing up in the world is your road map to success.

Tips:

1. Only the real you can attract the life that you want.
2. You will not go wrong by utilizing your natural gifts and talents.
3. Focus more on your personal values than those of society.
4. Attempting to protect yourself not only keeps others out, it also locks you in.

Scripture references:

Proverbs 16:9, John 16:13, Galatians 1:10

DECISION MAKING

Making a choice is not always an easy task. It is subjective according to your beliefs. You may consciously choose one route and a colleague will choose the opposite. It's essential to look at the reasons for your decisions. If the reason is rooted in fear or even in a dysfunctional dynamic such as neglect or abuse, then it is likely a bad choice. However, if you find yourself continually desiring a thing and it represents growth, stability, and positivity, it is likely a good choice. Timing is always a factor, so just because we want something does not mean it is a good decision at that time. Weighing the pros and cons is practical, but it is not wise to neglect your feelings and intuition. Decisions should be both practical and intuitive. Also, if the decision directly affects loved ones, it is important to consider their feelings. You have free will, so choose wisely.

Tips:

1. Create a plan to ensure a successful outcome. Re-evaluate the plan as needed.
2. Spend time alone for confirmation.
3. When unsure, make the choice that leans toward the fruition of your ultimate goal.
4. Have faith and see it through. Indecisiveness causes confusion, and confusion leads to unnecessary stress.
5. In the words of Albert Einstein, "Insanity is doing the same thing over and over and expecting different results."
6. Talk to a therapist or counselor to help put things into perspective.

Scripture references:

Deuteronomy 31:6, Ephesians 5:15-17, Proverbs 13:12-18

Dark Energies

We are spiritual beings, and our life on earth is a spiritual war. Light versus dark energies are at play; it is your spiritual nature versus your human nature. Whenever you feel the need to make changes for the better, an opposing energy in the form of a thought will enter your mind. An example of this is when a person feels guilt and remorse for marital infidelity and wants to confess everything to their spouse, but then thinks that by confessing, they will put the spouse in a position of power which will result in their loss of influence. The fleshly, carnal mind is selfish and confined and wants you to be safe, while your spirit wants expansion. This is indicative of spiritual warfare. In the example above, the unfaithful partner is more concerned with power than being honest with their spouse. Light energies are rooted in the Divine and include honesty, trust, acceptance, freedom, peace, intuition, accountability, and love.

On the contrary, dark energies are rooted in carnality and show up in the form of lies, obsession, possession, defensiveness, pride and ego, jealousy, fear, addictions, etc. Dark energies, if not managed early on, can lead to your demise.

Tips:

1. The key to transformation is to get beyond your physical reality.
2. Pray and ask for help on your spiritual journey.
3. Find a balance between your human nature and your spiritual nature. Too much or too little of anything affects natural balance.
4. Trust in the light of the Divine and follow the path even if you are unsure.

Scripture references:

Ephesians 6:11, Galatians 5:16-17, Romans 8:7-13

Spending Time Alone

Between work, family, and friends, it is sometimes difficult to find alone time. Spending time alone is a time for reflection and retrospection. It is a significant component of your life's journey. Connection to oneself happens when there are no distractions; you will gain clarity and find answers to the questions you seek. Other people's opinions and views can influence your thoughts and ultimately your choices. While great advice is a blessing, bad advice is a hindrance. Prioritize the relationship with yourself because no one knows you better than you.

Tips:

1. Be intentional about carving out time for yourself daily; it is a form of self-love.
2. Periodically, it is good to disconnect from your cell phone, television, and social media.
3. Take a walk in nature or sit outside at night when the world has slowed down.

Scripture references:

Proverbs 27:19, 2 Corinthians 13:5, Matthew 6:6

Divine Intervention

Ascension to new levels requires you to step out of your comfort zone and do what feels uncomfortable. Many people are spiritually immature and some simply refuse to make changes in their lives; consequently, they tend to repeat the same patterns. At times, God will step in and shake things up. One example of this is when speeding while driving under the influence results in a car crash. The car is demolished, but you have no idea how you survived the crash without a scratch on your body. The accident was an utterly humbling experience, and consequently, you no longer drink and drive. Things happen to teach you a spiritual lesson, prevent you from going down a certain path, or help push you toward your destiny. Certain events in your life are divinely guided for your growth and benefit. Therefore, if an unexpected event happens, whether pleasant or unpleasant, it is a good time to activate your faith.

Tips:

1. Pray and take steps toward spiritual growth.
2. Trust in the flow of your life.
3. Believe in a power greater than yourself.
4. Be open to change.

Scripture references:

Proverbs 16:9, Jeremiah 29:11, Proverbs 3:5

Soul Family vs. Blood Family

I frequently hear the saying, "Blood is thicker than water." Some people were raised to believe that family members should receive loyalty and unlimited forgivable passes, above all others, no matter their behavior. Bonds built with family members are some of the strongest connections you will ever have. On the same token, many people have terrible relationships with family members, including their parents. Sometimes toxicity is a family trait. Thus, if a neighbor is trustworthy and a sibling is a thief, then it would be wise to choose the neighbor to watch over your belongings. Every person has the responsibility to examine their behaviors. Judgment is not respective to the family name.

Tips:

1. Value and embrace relationships with a foundation of love and support.
2. Protect your energy and create healthy boundaries.
3. Be grateful for all the people who have made a positive impact on your life.

Scripture references:

Mark 3:35, Matthew 12:46-50, John 1:12

Honest Communication

Communication can be tough, especially when you are not accustomed to self-expression or if the topic of communication is in opposition to what someone else wants or believes. Honest communication is the foundation for the resolution of issues, and resolving issues is a major component of a successful relationship. Sincerity goes a long way, so even if people are not receptive to your opinions or feelings, your honesty will be appreciated. Be sure to include the full truth and not half-truths. For example, advising your partner that you were fired from your job but not disclosing the reason why is not honest communication. Not only does full transparency provide clarity, but it also builds and rebuilds trust. All involved parties will have a better understanding moving forward.

Tips:

1. If you are unable to verbally communicate, sincere written communication will suffice.
2. Communicate your true feelings with love and consideration for others.
3. Pay attention to your body language and make eye contact.
4. Listen to understand and not to respond.

Scripture references:

Ephesians 4:15, Luke 6:45, Psalm 19:14

Set Clear Boundaries

Setting personal boundaries is a crucial component of creating the life you want. Not only is it a form of self-care, but it also protects your energy. You are in control of your life and what you allow in your space. If someone does something to make you feel uncomfortable, it is your responsibility to express your needs so that adjustments can be made accordingly. Not speaking up to avoid possible disagreements and allowing others to make decisions for you illustrate poor boundaries. Examples of setting clear boundaries include advising your family and friends not to call you after a certain time during the night, not allowing others to make condescending comments towards you, and asking others to respect your privacy. You are valuable and what you need matters. It is never too late to re-evaluate your relationship dynamics.

Tips:

1. Understand that it is okay to say no.
2. Teach people how to treat you.
3. Respect other people's boundaries as well. If you are unsure about something, ask them.
4. Pay attention to a person's actions. You will be able to gauge their likes and dislikes.

Scripture references:

Proverbs 4:23, Matthew 5:37, Proverbs 25:17

Examine Yourself

You were chosen to be here on this Earth to live this life at this time. The life that you live starts with who you are at your core. Every person that you encounter in your lifetime will experience some aspect of you. You get to decide how you are remembered. I personally want to be remembered as someone who is dependable, honest, and caring. The way you show up in this world depends on how you see yourself and your ability to deal with adversity. It is important to hold yourself to a higher standard to experience the best life has to offer. By the same token, it is only then that you will expect the best for yourself. So, I ask, are you proud of the person you are today?

Tips:

1. Feed your soul by reading and listening to self-help books.
2. Be receptive to constructive criticism.
3. Be mindful of pride, conceit, or boastfulness.
4. Self-examination is a lifelong practice.

Scripture references:

1 Corinthians 11:28-32, Lamentations 3:40, Matthew 7:12

Hurt People, Hurt People

Many people are walking around with unhealed traumatic wounds negatively affecting those who are closest to them. As a result of previously being mistreated, they have created mental and emotional blockages that have diminished their faith. Operating strictly from their ego, whether knowingly or unknowingly, they will use tactics such as blaming, lying, manipulation, gaslighting, and other toxic behaviors as a form of protection. Withholding is a common example. A person will withhold information or pretend to not understand something so that they do not have to engage in conversation. It is extremely difficult to connect with people who are unwilling to be vulnerable. These behaviors only keep their soul stuck in a dark place and prevent the opportunity to build loving relationships. The struggle is evident in dynamics wherein people bring significantly more drama and victimhood instead of optimism and accountability.

When a person is unable to reciprocate positive energy, you are left feeling drained, alone, confused, and misunderstood. Someone else's baggage can easily be projected onto you.

Tips:

1. Set clear boundaries.
2. Be mindful of who you let into your space.
3. You cannot love the toxic behavior out of a person; they must choose to invest in their own healing.
4. Do not be a participant in someone's mind games.
5. Shine a light on the truth for healing.

Scripture references:

Matthew 7:6, Psalm 51:10, Proverbs 18:14

Breaking Generational Curses

A generational curse is a term used to describe unhealthy behavioral patterns that were not addressed within the family unit and are noticeable in the following generation(s). Building a legacy is not merely relative to financial stability but also mental and emotional stability. Some examples of generational curses include substance abuse, poverty, incest, dietary concerns, and family secrets. These are spiritual strongholds that have become normalized. Your habits are a major component of the foundation laid for your growth and the progress of your lineage. For instance, if there is a family history of obesity, heart disease, or even domestic violence, you may be the chosen one to break the cycle. It calls for a lifestyle change. As you identify your personal areas of opportunity, educate yourself accordingly.

Breaking unhealthy patterns is not easy but can be done; it takes commitment to change. Small steps will make a large impact in the long run.

Tips:

1. Imagine the life you want and create it.
2. Lead by example.
3. Commit to your spiritual development.
4. Determine if certain habits are yours or if you picked them up from someone.

Scripture references:

Ephesians 6:12, Deuteronomy 24:16, Proverbs 22:6

Seed Time and Harvest

Have you ever heard the sayings, "You reap what you sow" and "What goes around comes around?" These quotes simply explain the concept of cause and effect also known as karma. When you have good intentions and put your time, energy, and effort into a project, you will be rewarded for it. God sees all, so even when you feel that you have done all that you can do and you still do not see the fruits of your labor, don't be discouraged. You have already planted the seed; therefore, you will receive the fruits of your labor. Your harvest may take some time and may even show up in unexpected ways. It's important to stay in a spirit of gratitude and know that whatever is meant for you will be.

Tips:

1. Remain positive and faithful.
2. Expect and be receptive to good things that enter your life.
3. It is not wise to continue to put effort into barren soil (dead-end jobs, situations, or relationships).
4. There is a season for all things. Use your intuition as your guide.

Scripture references:

Galatians 6:7-9, 2 Corinthians 9:6, Proverbs 11:18

THERE IS MORE THAN ENOUGH

Having a scarcity mindset is a limiting belief that there is not enough of a resource, and your actions are centered around this belief. A scarcity mindset will be evident in behaviors such as settling in relationships and jobs as well as constantly having the feeling that the "pickings are slim" or that there is not enough to go around. One example is making impulsive buying decisions because you believe there is a limited number of items available. Another example is wanting to relocate to a certain geographic region, but you believe that it's impossible to make a certain amount of money to live comfortably in that area. These thoughts cause you to hold on to things too tightly out of fear that you will be left with nothing. As a result, you will find yourself anxious, angry, stressed, afraid to take risks, and laser-focused on lack instead of abundance.

You are now in survival mode with no peace. Thankfully, this can change. Shift your mindset to focus on sufficiency, and when opportunities present themselves, only accept the best options for you. This world offers more than enough for you to prosper.

Tips:

1. Believe in the possibilities of life.
2. Love yourself and know your worth.
3. Learn techniques on how to plan for long-term goals.
4. Push through the frustration and stay optimistic.
5. Give to others as an act of gratitude.

Scripture references:

2 Corinthians 8:14, John 10:10, Luke 6:38

A Guilty Conscience

A guilty conscience is the result of having said or done something you later regret because you felt it was wrong. Maybe you started a rumor or said something hurtful to someone, cheated in a relationship, or lied to a friend. This has happened to all of us at one time or another. A guilty conscience is your spirit alerting you that correction is needed. Guilt can be paralyzing and cause feelings of embarrassment, making you want to hide and seclude yourself in social settings. If your wrongdoing affects another person, then it is necessary to sincerely apologize to that person as soon as possible. Unfortunately, in certain situations, you may not get the opportunity to apologize. If so, it is even more important to forgive yourself. Sincere apologies require vulnerability, especially if you value your relationship with that person. When guilt is present because of a broken vow or commitment to yourself, give yourself grace, dust yourself off, and continue moving forward.

Tips:

1. You must understand the reason for your action. It is a lesson to be learned.
2. No one is perfect, so do not be too hard on yourself, but don't use imperfection as an excuse to not address the issue.
3. Address your personal feelings and those of others sooner rather than later.
4. Reflect on your wrongdoing, learn from it, and forgive yourself.

Scripture references:

Proverbs 28:13, Romans 3:23, Psalms 32:1-6

Don't Be Greedy

There is a societal debate on whether wanting to make more money is a bad thing. Personally, I believe the desire for expansion is a remarkable thing and I encourage everyone to strive for financial freedom and security. We all need money to survive, and there is nothing wrong with wanting more to enhance your life. However, if your wants are extremely excessive and motivated simply by the desire to get more, then it becomes greed. Greed is rooted in selfishness and feeds the ego. Wanting something for all the wrong reasons will cause you to not appreciate what you currently have been blessed with. Examples are marrying for money rather than love or taking more than is offered to you when given the opportunity. A constant desire for material things should not outweigh the desire for honorable deeds, meaningful relationships, or self-respect. Keep your intentions pure because greed can lead you down a dark path that results in a lost soul.

Tips:

1. Join a community outreach program to support the less fortunate.
2. Grow in your spirituality by practicing meditation and journaling to help discover a deeper connection with yourself.
3. Incorporate more ways of giving into your life.
4. Place more value on experiences than on spending.

Scripture references:

1 Ecclesiastes 5:10, 1 John 2:16, 1 Timothy 6:9-10

Feelings of Jealousy

Jealousy is an emotion that arises when another person's presence or accomplishments make you feel inferior to them. It is an emotional trigger that stems from an underlying issue of low self-esteem and insecurities. The ego is activated, which leads to comparing and competing with others. One way to spot jealousy is if you find yourself attempting to outshine someone. The hidden competition causes internal turmoil that will only make you feel worse when you discover that you are the only opponent. Every person has been blessed with individual characteristics, gifts, and talents. These traits were designed specifically for you and should not be compared to others. You are loved for being you; therefore, embrace your uniqueness and the feelings of jealousy will begin to fade.

Tips:

1. Celebrate other's accomplishments.
2. Give thanks to the Creator for your existence.
3. Your self-esteem will improve as you strive to become the best version of yourself.
4. Share your gifts and talents with the world.

Scripture references:

Exodus 20:17, James 3:14-16, Proverbs 14:30

Taking Accountability

Avoidance and "sweeping things under the rug" in hopes that they will go away is wishful thinking. While it may seem to be handled for the moment, if this pattern of behavior continues, sooner or later it will rear its head again. Being accountable means being responsible for your choices. True accountability addresses the action, the reason for the action, and how the action affects others. For example, being able to admit to someone that you failed to keep an appointment because you were unprepared or nervous and sincerely apologizing for how it made them feel is true accountability. Not only does accountability build your character and make you proud of the person that you see in the mirror, but others will also respect you for it. On the other hand, when you shy away from being accountable, people will not take you seriously, and your relationships will suffer because you will be viewed as untrustworthy.

Becoming a person of integrity through accountability gives you the credibility needed to persevere in your endeavors.

Tips:

1. Accept that no one is perfect. We all make mistakes, so when you mess up, get up and try again.
2. Excuses and accountability cannot coexist in the same conversation.
3. It is not always someone else's fault.
4. It's easy to be confident in your abilities when you lead with honesty and truth.
5. Accept constructive criticism.

Scripture references:

James 4:17, James 5:16, Romans 14:12

Enabling Is Not Helping

Enablers usually have good intentions. They are very supportive, and they like to help others, especially loved ones. The problem is that they have a hard time saying no to others who continually get themselves in unfavorable predicaments. In particular, many parents have a hard time releasing their adult children into the world to learn life's lessons. Instead, they bail them out financially and make decisions for them. While it is commendable to have compassion for others, it is imperative to set boundaries for your own health and well-being. Taking on too many responsibilities is stressful, and stress negatively affects your mental and physical health. Also, enablers put themselves in a position to be taken advantage of due to their poor boundaries. They subconsciously stunt the growth of and support the poor decisions of those that they continue to rescue.

You must allow them to learn the lessons of life. It is only when a person can truly feel the consequences of their actions that they make the necessary changes.

Tips:

1. It is important to put yourself first.
2. The word "no" is not a bad thing. Sometimes what works for others does not work for you and that's okay.
3. If you find yourself complaining about constantly helping someone, but you continue to do so, you need to evaluate the reason you are unable to say no.
4. You are not helping someone if you keep doing things for them that they can do for themselves.

Scripture references:

2 Thessalonians 3:10, Galatians 6:7, Proverbs 19:19

Surrender

Whether you are dealing with a partner who is not on the same page as you, being suddenly laid off from your job, experiencing loss from a natural disaster, or hearing the diagnosis of an illness, etc., there will be times when the unexpected happens. During times of unforeseen circumstances, your life will pivot in another direction. The best thing for your mental and emotional health is to surrender to outcomes that are beyond your control. Surrender means not fighting against or resisting your new reality. Learn to adapt and redirect your focus on how to move forward. With acceptance comes peace; you can make the best out of the situation. The past is gone, your reality has changed, and there is only now.

Tips:

1. Decide from the moment of today what your new life looks like.
2. Stay faithful and know that a higher power is at play.
3. Find the positivity and creativity that comes with all things new.
4. Guard your mind from negativity, activate your faith, and believe in the positive outcome of your current situation.
5. Seek counsel from others that have experienced and successfully overcome similar events.

Scripture references:

2 Corinthians 5:7, Psalms 46:10, 2 Timothy 1:7

Ask for Help

There will be times when you have a vision that you want to pursue or you are faced with a situation that you aren't prepared for. You may find you have no idea where to start. You need to ask for help. As you seek information, the right people will cross your path. Many have come before you and many will come after you. People are resources, and the world is filled with capable people and organizations to assist with your needs. For instance, if you are interested in changing careers, ask around for networking opportunities with people in that industry. Don't worry about those who may refuse or turn you away. Just as some won't help, others will. You only need to take a different route.

Tips:

1. Find a mentor.
2. Get out, make introductions, and meet new people.
3. Be humble and don't allow pride to get in the way.
4. Be willing to learn and take notes on the information received.

Scripture references:

Matthew 7:7, Hosea 4:6, James 4:10

SELF-SABOTAGE

So, you want something but tend to find reasons not to pursue the desires of your heart. Self-sabotaging behaviors include negative self-talk, procrastination, and indecision. Thinking that you are not good enough causes you to pursue things that you can win or obtain with little to no effort (low-hanging fruit). Examples include dating only people who need you, under-charging for your services, or applying for jobs that you are overqualified for. Having a "take what I can get" attitude prevents you from reaching your full potential. When negativity creeps into your mind, you will think of all the reasons why something will not happen instead of focusing on the possibilities. You must train your mind because negative thinking can prevent you from acting and even divert your attention toward unhealthy distractions. You must first believe that it can happen, no matter the external factors.

Deep down, there may be a fear of failure. Fear can be paralyzing, so remember that there is no failure, only lessons.

Tips:

1. Speak positive affirmations to combat negative self-talk.
2. Keep a daily journal of your thoughts and actions. Be intentional toward your goals.
3. Surround yourself with positive people who encourage you.
4. Keep a journal to write down your thinking patterns. This will show you what you are thinking about and allow you to incorporate positive thinking.
5. Focus on healing any old wounds.

Scripture references:

John 8:32, Romans 12:2, Philippians 4:13

Making Assumptions

The easiest way to bring strife into your relationships is to make assumptions about someone. For instance, we shouldn't assume that all attractive people are intelligent or that all men cheat. If your assumptions are based on gossip, then take the information with a grain of salt. Try not to let hearsay influence what you believe. Keep in mind that people lie. If you are familiar with the character of a person, then trust your instincts. Still, try to confirm the details of a situation. It is fair to give someone the benefit of the doubt; however, a person's behavior can lead you toward the truth. Every situation is based on its own merit, and what happened yesterday is not guaranteed to happen today. If you do not know something to be true, don't assume.

Tips:

1. Think for yourself and use your own discernment.
2. Watch out for manipulative people.
3. Pray and ask for clarity.
4. Keep an open mind.
5. If you are misjudged, brush it off, and let your character speak for itself.
6. Initiate a conversation for clarity.

Scripture references:

Ecclesiastes 10:13-15, Matthew 7:15-20, Proverbs 18:2

People Pleasing

People pleasers have a pattern of putting the needs of others before their own. One example that you may be a people pleaser is if your friends suggest going out for pizza and you agree, even though pizza gives you heartburn. Nevertheless, you eat it anyway. There is a need to avoid conflict and be liked, accepted, and validated by others. Furthermore, people pleasers attract takers, and takers continuously accept offerings without reciprocity. If all your time is spent making others happy, then that leaves nothing for you. As time passes, you will begin to feel depleted and ultimately develop feelings of resentment. You only have one life to live, and it's time to make the necessary adjustments for your happiness. When you start to speak up for yourself, the takers will begin to say that you are difficult to deal with. Ignore the blasphemy and continue to live for you.

Tips:

1. Verbally express your wants and needs.
2. Participate in things that make you happy.
3. Make your needs a priority.
4. Set firm boundaries and say no when necessary.

Scripture references:

Galatians 1:10, Colossians 3:23, Proverbs 29:25

EGO

Your ego is the part of you that is based on the beliefs of the body and mind. It is a false sense of self and is relative to one's image, pride, social status, material wealth, etc. Egotistical dynamics include making decisions based on other people's perceptions of you, competing with others, hiding your true nature, and ignoring your morals for external validation. The ego seeks self-gratification and wants to win at all costs. It is in direct conflict with your spirit. Our spirituality teaches us about the ego versus the soul and how they are on two opposite ends of the spectrum, with one (the ego) based on external factors and the other (the soul) based on your inner man. While your ego is there to protect you, it also keeps you from spiritual development and will cause you to miss out on blessings. Succumbing to your ego is a culprit of manifestation. Your intuition comes from your true self and is your divine guidance.

It will lead you toward a life of love, happiness, peace, and freedom from bondage.

Tips:

1. Listen to your intuition and follow its direction.
2. Practice vulnerability.
3. Take accountability for your actions.
4. Surround yourself with authentic people who love and support the real you.
5. Be honest with yourself and others about your life's journey.

Scripture references:

Philippians 2:3, James 3:16, John 4:24

TRUSTING OTHERS

My question to you is this: Is trust something to be earned, or is it given freely until proven otherwise? In my opinion, extending the grace of trust is commendable and creates the opportunity to build meaningful relationships with others. On the other hand, those who feel trust must be earned have usually endured an unpleasant experience regarding the issue of trust. The decision to trust someone should not be based on the actions of another person or the opinions of others.

For example, some people trust men but do not trust women (or vice versa) because one parent was unfaithful and the other spouse suffered. Again, this belief comes from an experience and internalizing the pain of another. It is wise to keep your expectations realistic when dealing with human beings; no one is perfect, and depending on the internal battles of a person, they may violate your trust.

This is why we should not put our trust in man. Shift your focus to a higher power. By doing so, you will have the discernment to know who is trustworthy. You will heal from traumas, and you will be able to move forward without baggage into a new cycle of life.

Tips:

1. Give everyone the benefit of the doubt until you receive further information.
2. Listen to your intuition. When something seems or feels off, it usually is.
3. Recognize familiar patterns of behavior for clarity.
4. Don't worry; things done in the dark will come to light eventually.
5. Untrustworthy people are dealing with unhealed traumas. Try not to take it personally.
6. Making someone prove themselves comes from a place of insecurity.

Scripture references:

Psalm 112:7, Jeremiah 17:7, Proverbs 3:5

Dealing with Temptation

The feeling of desiring something that is not good for you or your life's vision best describes temptation. Temptation can be anything that your better judgment would steer clear of such as gossiping, substance abuse, lying, unhealthy eating, cheating, and stealing. This is an example of feeding your flesh versus your soul. The feeling of reluctance that comes alongside temptation cautions your decision. We are all guaranteed to face temptation, but because of individual levels of maturity as well as individual strengths and weaknesses, the results of surrender will vary. What may be tempting to one person can create feelings of repulsion in someone else. It takes spiritual discipline and a strong sense of self to win the battle. Succumbing to temptation comes with consequences and will bring feelings of guilt. If this happens, it should be acknowledged as an area of opportunity.

As you continue to grow spiritually and stand firm in who you are, listening to that small still voice from within will become second nature.

Tips:

1. Know your personal challenges and offer self-correction.
2. Stay away from people and environments that cause you to backslide.
3. Reject the temptation to build your self-confidence.
4. Give yourself grace for mistakes and move forward. Never give up on yourself.

Scripture references:

1 Corinthians 10:13, Matthew 26:41, Luke 4:13

COMPASSION FOR OTHERS

You are called to have compassion and empathy for others as an act of kindness for your fellow man. This includes the homeless person standing on the street corner with a sign asking for help. It is easy to be concerned only with the lives of your inner circle of family and friends while dismissing the welfare of others. We must make a conscious effort to spread love, even to outsiders and strangers, and especially to those who are less fortunate or without loved ones. The Golden Rule teaches us to treat others as we would like to be treated. Even if you believe that a person deserves misfortune because of their actions, it is not your place to cast judgment. Try putting yourself in their shoes. We all desire support, kindheartedness, and compassion despite our faults. Something as simple as a smile, compliment, or pleasant attitude can brighten someone's day.

Tips:

1. Pay it forward. Whenever someone does something nice for you, repay the kindness to someone else.
2. You are blessed to be a blessing.
3. Operating in a spirit of gratefulness opens your heart to give.
4. Cast down thoughts that prevent you from helping others.

Scripture references:

1 John 3:17, Matthew 7:12, Colossians 3:12

ILLUSIONS

The mind is very powerful and can create illusions based on what you want, what you think about, and what you see. When the reality of a situation is in direct opposition to what you wholeheartedly believe to be true, you may be in denial. You can desire something so much that you ignore the warnings that are right in front of your face. One example is when you love someone blindly and ignore red flags like constant arguments, infidelity, and failure to communicate. You stay in an unhealthy relationship because you "love them." Another example is that you desire to move up within the company that you work for and have discussions with your boss who promises you a promotion. Five years later, you are still in the same position while the company continues to hire and promote other employees. Your beliefs, as well as manipulation by others, can prevent you from seeing and accepting the truth of a situation.

Accepting harsh truths can be very painful and most times it means that you will have to accept endings to the very things in which you have placed your identity. Finding out that everything you thought to be true was a lie can shatter your entire world. Allow the truth to set you free because fighting for something that is not real is exhausting and counterproductive. Thank God for clarity because lies will only keep you in bondage.

Tips:

1. Remember that your real identity comes from within—not from external factors.
2. Periodically take time for yourself to re-evaluate your circumstances.
3. Stay positive because negative thoughts affect your beliefs.
4. Pay attention to red flags and move toward situations that align more with your desires.

Scripture references:

1 Peter 5:8, Isaiah 44:20, Luke 8:17

Follow the Path Given to You

Creative ideas will periodically come to your mind as inspiration for progress in any area of your life. Your creative thoughts are unique to you and can be viewed as a road map toward your destiny. For instance, if you love to cook and create recipes and people enjoy your food, you have a passion for cooking. These ideas are worth pursuing and are authentic to you. Many times, we talk ourselves out of pursuing ideas because we lack the discipline needed, or we don't believe we are capable. You are worthy and already equipped with everything you need to get you to the next step. Be open and trust the process. As you present yourself to the world, you will continue to discover new and exciting things about yourself. You will also take more chances. With increased confidence and continued internal guidance, you will succeed.

Tips:

1. Take risks. If you are afraid, do it anyway.
2. Keep your mind guarded against negative self-talk.
3. You are exactly what someone needs.
4. Don't compare yourself to others because you are not like anyone else.

Scripture references:

Genesis 1:27, Psalm 139:13-14, Matthew 10:30

DEALING WITH DIFFICULT PEOPLE

At some point in your life, you will encounter a person who is hard to deal with. Difficult people cause confusion, are selfish, and like to argue. Most times they are ignorant of the things they argue about, yet they are extremely defensive. It feels like their only existence is to make your life a living hell. People with these characteristics can be emotionally unstable and unpredictable. They see themselves as victims and feel that their problems exist because of everyone else except their own choices. Ironically, they live for drama and secretly thrive on dark energy because it is subconsciously familiar. You may have tried everything within your power to have a peaceful existence with this person, but their conversation is negative and so is their outlook on life. You can't change them, so don't try. Keep your distance if possible.

However, if you must deal with them, I recommend keeping your interactions to a minimum because it is your responsibility to protect your peace.

Tips:

1. Try not to provoke them. It will only turn out badly.
2. If it is a loved one, stay positive and recommend they talk to a counselor or therapist.
3. Listen to them.
4. Pray for their deliverance from whatever is bothering them.

Scripture references:

Proverbs 15:1, Proverbs 22:24, Psalms 34:18

Be Intentional

To be intentional, you must first know what you want and why you want it. Being intentional causes you to make conscious decisions that lead toward a desired path. There is a difference between making a choice that's best for you versus letting your circumstances choose for you. This is why you must get to know the real you. Your internal desires, not your external circumstances, and not the desires of others will guide you. Only you will know how valuable something is to you. When you communicate your intentions, you are better understood and can visualize the direction you are headed.

A second meaning for intention has to do with one's state of being when acting. Sometimes it's not solely about the action itself but the reasoning behind it. For instance, keeping secrets due to deception compared to keeping secrets for protection from harm should be viewed differently.

When your heart is in the right place and you have pure intentions, you are on the right track. Stay faithful and true.

Tips:

1. There is a saying, "If you don't stand for something, you will fall for anything." It is true. Take heed.
2. Write down your plans and make a daily routine.
3. Acknowledge your most important relationships.
4. Trust yourself.

Scripture references:

James 4:17, Proverbs 14:2, Habakkuk 2:2

Conclusion

I hope that you have enjoyed reading *The Gift of Wisdom: Encouragement for the Soul*. Some topics were chosen by God through revelation, and some were requested by friends and family. Each synopsis was written to help identify areas of opportunity for spiritual growth and provide inspiration along the way.

The recommended tips are good starting points that can be applied to your life. The bible scriptures are a bonus and can further put things into perspective. We are responsible for our own lives. YOU can create the life that you want. Distorted thinking patterns, unhealed traumas, and a lack of knowledge keep us stuck in familiar situations. Our spirituality allows us to tap into a world beyond our current circumstances. Getting beyond your current reality is the key.

This book only serves as a guide and is solely my opinion. I was led to write this book because I truly believe it can help someone. While every topic may not be something that you are currently dealing with, I ask that you take what you need, leave what you don't, and share the wisdom with someone who may need encouragement.

Wisdom lasts forever and can never be taken from you. This is my gift to you. Thank you again for your support.

With love,
Donna Sims

www.ingramcontent.com/pod-product-compliance
Lightning Source LLC
LaVergne TN
LVHW011733060526
838200LV00051B/3166